I0458095

174 Edgewood

Charlotte Lit Press
Charlotte Center for Literary Arts, Inc.

PO Box 18607
Charlotte, NC 28218

charlottelit.org/press

Copyright 2025 by Barbara Campbell
All rights reserved

Cover image by Serdar Yazıcı
Author photo by Dannye Romine Powell

ISBN: 978-1-960558-13-8

PROUD MEMBER

[clmp]

COMMUNITY OF LITERARY MAGAZINES & PRESSES
W W W . C L M P . O R G

174 Edgewood

Poems

Barbara Campbell

CHARLOTTE**LIT**
P R E S S

Contents

Preface

Some say that when you die you meet again those who've gone before. I'd be so glad to see my husband first. But now that I'm near the age she was when she passed away, I can't help but wonder if my mother will be the one to greet me? Will I have to hear again all the things she had to put up with—seven living children, four miscarriages, frustration that she didn't have time for her art? The mouths that needed constant feeding, the bodies to clothe and ferry, the noses she had to wipe? I wonder what she might say about the booze, about the resilience of her progeny, about all that got handed down. Would she fault me for the ways I've followed her, the stories I've told? I suppose we get what we give, something she might remind me of. I have two sons, one a writer, one a psychologist, and I know full well that I'm likely to become the protagonist in the stories they tell. If they remember me as difficult, I hope they'll also remember the love. One thing is certain, should I meet them at the pearly gates one day, they won't have to answer to me for anything at all.

174 Edgewood

An old photo of our house shows
windows blindfolded with wood,
crumbled brick steps leading to dirt-
streaked door. Gone from either side,
the hollies—one short, the other tall—
that Dad, after his third highball,
used as a toilet.

Above, the bedroom window
where I watched my older sister betray
me with the boy who, just a day before,
had given me my first kiss—his lips full
and tight like hot dogs, his breath moist
with scotch and Dentyne.

Across the driveway the yellow birch
where I built a plywood perch for playing
Tarzan's Jane. No homewrecker,
me, I was in this one for flight.

We wore our house like a turtle does
a shell. We bruised and rollicked
through childhood, marking that place
the way a cat rubs her owner's leg.
When we left, the house was razed
and replaced by Edgewood Estates.

Seventy years on, memories of 174
worry through my brain's coils
like a flip flop that wriggles its way
up the landfill's muddy layers
and through the golf course's green
cover to rattle players on the ninth tee.

I only need to see the shot, and I'm home.

How My Parents Met and Lived Unhappily Ever After

The picture of the Gilbert & Sullivan Troupe shows her ruby-lustre lips smiling at him as he, kneeling, hands her yellow tulips. She's a lively village maid full of wit, flirting with the lead baritone, whom, her story goes, she kicked to get a cigarette. He was so smitten he wouldn't stop calling till she gave in. We kids loved her telling this story, the two of them, so young, enraptured with each other in a way none of us had ever seen.

Could she have imagined that during the first decade of their life together she would bear seven children, that the relief she'd feel at cocktail hour could be prolonged throughout the day with sips, then gulps from bottles hidden in the clothes hamper and library sofa? Could he have imagined his relief as he boarded the early train into the city to his law practice, days broken by long lunches and then martinis in the club car home? Could he have expected her anger when she picked him up at the station, the way she raged about her day gone from bad to worse, which kids needed spanking, how he should stay home one day to see how hard her life really was?

Hennessey in the Hamper

No Nancy Drew
no spying on the boy,
next door, we have
a better game—
snooping to find
where Mom hides
her bottles. We notch
the liquid levels,
put them back
for her return. Here
she comes again—

Hennessy in the hamper,
snow-booted vermouth,
Gilbey's in the linens—
Cold sandwiches
for supper tonight.

They Must Have Loved Sex

That's the one sure thing we now know,
though the sounds from their bedroom
were foreign at first, and worrisome.
But soon enough, it would grow quiet.
We'd hurry back to our rooms to avoid
getting caught outside during "naptime."
Then it was over. The afternoon begun,
we'd forget about the grunts and squeals.

I was eight when our oldest sister finally
gave us *the talk*—our parents were doing
what people did to make babies. She told us
how the male had a thing he'd put into
a woman's hole, the place where later a baby
would pop out.

For so many years after, I imagined sex
like a piggy bank: Drop in a quarter,
turn it over and shake out coins. Imagine
my disappointment that first time—my boyfriend's
whispered moans, me wishing I were back
in my room shaking out the change.

A Bi-Polar Christmas

O Come All Ye Faithful we'd sing every Christmas
morning as we marched into the living room

to find our hoped-for presents under the tree.
But that year, our manic mother, like a kid bursting

with the thrill of her secret, hurried the six of us—
four girls and two boys, ages seventeen to six—up

the attic stairs to where, hunkering in the musty half-light,
like bison in a blizzard, were six antique bureaus—

walnut, mahogany, cherry—in various states of decay.
Gifts on no one's list. When I saw the top drawer

of mine had no bottom, I couldn't help but sneer, *I guess
it'll be easy to put away clothes.* When he couldn't find

the Tonka truck she'd promised, Parker, the youngest,
began to cry. We'd been raised to mask disappointment,

but she had no rein on her own: *I should have known not
to waste quality on selfish brats!* Off she stomped to her room

for the day, leaving Dad to preside over a silent lunch—
cold mashed potatoes, cold roast beef, cold apple pie.

For Kate Who Made the Sandwiches

It didn't take much
to set you in motion
you the fifth girl, born
so soon after the last one
the one they sent away.

The quick uptick
of pressure in the air
a broken glass
Mom's slurry words
and you'd spool
through the kitchen
slapping

Velveeta, bologna, peanut butter
and marshmallow fluff
on Wonder Bread
shush and hurry
our little brothers outside
to the secret spot

behind the lilac trees
where you'd sit them down
start a story and pass
them sandwiches
the heavy scent of lilacs
blanketing you on
the mossy, green lawn.

Dinner at Friede's Tavern

Dinner at Friede's! our father would pronounce. A rare
treat for the three older girls and our mother, just the thing
to lift us out of a weekend funk. To dine under lamplight
in the dark, oak-panelled restaurant was, to us, the height
of sophistication.

Dad made a big deal of ordering two martinis and three
Mickey Mouse cocktails with extra maraschino cherries.
And we'd try to mimic Mom daintily sipping her drink.
After two more rounds, and with plenty of flair, Dad ordered
the roast beef special for all, while Mom reminded us
to remember our manners and not gobble our food.

But all too soon Dad would snap his fingers and bellow,
Garçon, tee more martoonis, and we'd blush, hope to die
or at least disappear. Pray the food would come quickly
so Dad would shut up before what always happened
happened.

He'd begin to sneeze, one loud *kerchoof* after another,
muting the room and kindling stares until our waiter,
who knew the drill, brought on a silver tray two aspirins
which Dad washed down with the end of his drink
before paying the check for food we never got to finish.
He overtipped, slurred his thanks for the always fantastic
service, and we fled to the car vowing never again
as Dad jerked the wheel and Mom muttered her prayers.

But two months later, Dad would yell up the stairs,
Get dressed girls, let's go to Friede's. Connie would
rouge her cheeks, Ellie tug at her curls, and I
would strap on my Mary Janes just as fast as I could.

My Time with Tarzan

Around the age of eight or nine,
I'd climb the horse chestnut
in our front yard and wait
for Tarzan to swing by
on one of his tangled vines.
He'd land on my branch,
scoop me into his arms
and off we'd fly tree to tree—
God, the thrill of swooping
and gliding through the sky
with no fear of falling.
That summer of despair,
it was enough to soar
with him above our house—
up, up until we were alone
flying through the clouds
on our way toward the warm
and welcoming sun.

What We Did with Dad When Mom Was Drinking

Certain fall and winter weekends,
though we could never predict when,
Dad would take the six of us
to the Long Island Sound beach,
our mission—to keep the incoming tide
from covering the sandbar. Armed
with shovels, pails, driftwood, we'd dig
holding ponds and channels to reverse
the water's course back to sea,
quickening our work as the sound
advanced until, at last, it had its way—
as it always did—and we had to
call it quits. But not one of us doubted
that some weekend, maybe not the next,
but eventually, we would succeed.

Do not touch

the doctor told my mother.
I was six months old and sick
with pneumonia, when Mardett
took over my care. Rigid
as a pencil in her starched uniform,
she gloved her hands
to change my diapers,
to pull me up onto her lap
for my bottle—hers the only
touch I knew till year's end.

Decades later, Mother told me
the story, thanking me
for the vacation. What could I do
but laugh? From her, I'd learned
to suck things up. But her confession
helped me understand why school
dances gave me clammy palms,
why wrapping my limbs round
a lover's body felt foreign, why
I wanted sex finished the moment
it started. Now I know how
late arrivals and early departures
helped me avoid the friendly embraces
that left me feeling raw. And, maybe,
after all these years, I can finally see why,
when they laid my first child

in my arms, I couldn't have known
how to hold him, how to get him
to latch onto my breast. Why
I felt so relieved when, at last,
the nurse said, *Go ahead,*
give him a bottle.

The One They Gave Away

Fourth of seven, her brown curls bounced as she drifted—
always tiptoed, never talked—through a secret world

where only she could go. First, they thought she was deaf
but when she hummed Beethoven's Sixth and twirled

in sync, they had to face a deeper loss, a flaw
they couldn't fix. She was three when we took her

to a new home several states away. What a jolly
trip for us sisters, first restaurant, first hotel—

a kiss, a wave, a last farewell—for her, restrained
by two attendants, a scream, a cry, a final glimpse

and then we were six.

The Summer Our Mother Turned Catholic

We had just moved to the Lane's estate after leaving our sister far-away in a home for the mentally retarded. Mrs. Lane, a devout Catholic, consoled our mother, which seemed for us a respite from the last month's wailing and fighting. Mom bowed her head and fingered her new rosary, whispering Hail Marys for the forgiveness found in Christ's sacrifice of blood and flesh, while we were free to roam with the Lane's son, Nelson. Years later, Nelson would become a priest, but one day that summer, he led us to a rock-edged pond, dared us to drop our panties and jump in, which we did. Then we began splashing him. Enraged by our teasing, he caught a frog in each hand and threw one after the other again and again against the rocks until both had flattened into moist tangled lumps of skin, eyes and mossy blood, their lifeless bodies a reminder that no matter how she prayed, Mom could not keep us safe and our sister wasn't ever coming home.

Betrayal Pays a Winter Visit to Maine

So many of those early days
as a young wife and mother
seem a blurred film,
voice and lips out of sync.
Still, one scene remains crystal clear:
I'd taken my infant son on a trip
to visit my childhood home.
He was sick—stuffed up, fussy,
wanting nothing except for me
to hold him. But I had needs too.
I'd been baptized in a quip-spitting,
gin-sipping, take-no-prisoners tribe—
you gave it, you got it, and I
wanted it back. *Pneumonia,*
said the hospital nurse,
He'll have to spend the night.
My poor baby clung to the high rail
of his crib, nose swollen,
fever-flushed, his eyes wide with terror
as I picked up my purse and left,
his wail not a bit more horrifying
than my relief.

Half an Avocado and a Dollop of Hollandaise

My mother would set the small oval table
in the den overlooking the harbour
with her linens and semi-good china
and my father, back for lunch
from his law practice, would make
his one old fashioned and bring her
a goblet with water and crushed ice.
First the hot soup, then the boat-shaped
avocado with hollandaise puddling
its hollow. He'd talk about his latest case,
and she about the misdeeds of the grandkids
who called her *Nanny No No*.
She and my father were at their best.
He, revived by his cocktail and chat,
she at her most sober, playing the good wife.
And each time lunch went well,
she'd believe she could stop drinking.
And he'd believe she would.

She'd start pounding the horn before the Ford turned into the driveway

increasing her fusillade as she looped by our collapsed barn, working up to a continuous honk as she stopped out back by the kitchen door. *Get out here and unload these groceries, you lugs. Do I have to do everything?* Meet our Mom the queen, who disappeared as we six worker ants unloaded the car and ferried food to pantry— Wonder Bread, Hellman's, bologna. Her mood meant no jokes, snickers, sly looks. She had a knack for nosing out mockery that increased when she was on the sauce, an expression we picked up from Dad but didn't fully comprehend, though we avoided testing her fury through an elaborate network of warning tics, winks, and hand signals. How clever we thought we were. Though none of us clever enough to imagine that in our later years most of us would still be dealing with *the sauce*.

What really mattered the day the ambulance took you away

was not your screaming, though we were terrified,
huddled together on the back porch, screened
by the broken trellis. It wasn't the words
Dad whispered, *Dry her out,* or the men
in white coats who wrapped you
with your own arms. What horrified me
was that you grabbed your wedding portraits
from the mantle—you in your veil
with that slight smile I know now was sardonic,
and the one with you and Dad, pitchfork straight.
This is our marriage! you raved as you smashed
the frames and shredded the photos, and all I
could do was worry whether there was enough
Scotch tape and where could I find the right glass
to fix it all before you came back.

On a wild November day

tangled in the train
of a late hurricane
streets stricken with sheets
of sodden leaves, hurled sticks
I lied to my therapist
about the number of days
a week I don't drink
four, I said, not three,

a deceit that seemed no kin
to me as the words lined up
in my mouth and marched
themselves out as if
they had every right.

Later, bolstered by pals—
No big deal, you're fine—
I confessed to her machine
said to self *no more lies*
and hoped to mean it,

while outside, rain ended,
sun peeked through,
though weak and washed
clean of warmth and
filtered by stubborn clouds.

I Am the Woman in the Story 'A Woman in Love with a Bottle'

—not the actual woman but so much like her
I knew I had to hide it. The excitement before
a party—not the guests, but the first sip—
the tongue tingling, the throat deliciously warm,
the knowing there'll be another then another—

                                              And I'm off

greeting those I run into with genuine charm, wit.
Me fuelled with wine until—

and here the picture gets less pretty—

my words begin to slur,
I share secrets I shouldn't.
I wobble when I stand to clear the table. I'm on
the downturn and know it. But I can't stop. I forget
the words to my stories, the point to my jokes,

                              the way to the bathroom

which makes me think I owe my dead mother an apology.

She's played the foil in all my poems and stories and is the tie
that binds me and my siblings to the chaos of childhood.
But what turmoil have I unleashed on my family? My friends?

Do my sons and their wives talk about people I no longer see?
Do they notice how quickly after dinner I leave, how the perfume
I wear takes over a room? How much like my mother I am?

Carnage

Six siblings
gather at the beach
after a long separation.
Uneasy with each other,
they bristle like sun-burnt
skin beneath coarse linen.
Yoked by DNA and bad jokes
about their mother's drinking,
they circle at water's edge
and watch the tide
relinquish a jellyfish
with a crab trapped inside,
both weakened,
but still alive.

Goodbye to Maine

The 747 lumbers down the rutted runway gaining speed
for its lift and I begin my goodbyes—

Goodbye to my sisters and brothers, linked to me and
each other by accidents of birth and all the ways we pulled
together to survive.

Goodbye to the gallons of wine we drinkers drank and
the coffee downed by the sober.

Goodbye to the me who spent too much time acting as if
she were three.

Goodbye to the drunk we almost hit, his too-familiar
stumbling on the rocky shoulder, his waving a bottle for balance,
yelling *Get out of my way.*

Goodbye to our splendid Maine home where our
mother's ghost still hovers and to the golden summers we
children enjoyed before we learned the name for all that was
wrong.

Acknowledgements

With gratitude to the following publications in which several of these poems first appeared: *North Carolina Literary Review, Kakalak,* and *Black Coffee Review.*

And a special thanks to Kathie Collins and Paul Reali for their creation and support of Charlotte Lit, to Kathie for the creation of Poetry Chapbook Lab and her work as Press editor-in chief, to my mentor, esteemed poet Lola Haskins, the other poets who made this journey with me, and to the late Dannye Romine Powell, a longtime friend, adviser, and fabulous poet who encouraged me to start writing so many years ago.

About the Author

Barbara (Bobbie) Campbell began her career in New York where she worked for Oxford University Press and The New Yorker, though she doesn't like to admit as a secretary. In 1966, she moved to Charlotte, NC with her husband, where they raised their sons and made a permanent home. A dedicated member of Charlotte's writing community, Campbell served as associate editor of the *Red Clay Reader* series, editions 4 through 7. She loves to read, travel, take daily walks, sing in a choir, Zoom with her remaining siblings, visit with her sons and their families, laugh with friends and watch films that are dark, dramatic and disturbing. Campbell's poetry has appeared in *Rattle, Kakalak; Journey Within; Pinesong; The Southern Poetry Anthology, North Carolina; Poet Lore* and others. *174 Edgewood* is her first poetry collection.

www.ingramcontent.com/pod-product-compliance
Lightning Source LLC
Chambersburg PA
CBHW020814130626
46554CB00006B/2427